The Atlas Martyrs

by

Jean Olwen Maynard

To my parish priest, Fr Tony Sacré

All booklets are published thanks to the generous support of the members of the Catholic Truth Society

CATHOLIC TRUTH SOCIETY
PUBLISHERS TO THE HOLY SEE

CONTENTS

Early Years in France and Algeria 3

Priest in France - Monk in Algeria 28

Towards the End 49

Testament of Christian de Chergé 73

Sources 76

Note: The moving story of these seven Cistercian monks has now been vividly recorded in the award winning film *Of Gods and Men*, directed by Xavier Beauvois, and released in May 2010. Lauded by critics worldwide, the film won the 'Grand Prix' at the Cannes Films Festival that year.

Early Years in France and Algeria

Back in France the sky had never been so blue, the houses so gleaming white or the sunshine so glorious. The three little boys skipped merrily along the street leading from the Sacred Heart Church. Catechism class had gone well; Christian had answered all the questions correctly, as usual, so that cross old Fr Repeticci hadn't thrown one of his performances, and Mummy was pleased. Now they were going home to spend the rest of the afternoon playing at soldiers. Suddenly an eerie wailing noise broke out. None of the Europeans took any notice, but the Arabs - the dark, bearded men in long robes - immediately stopped what they were doing and, without the slightest fuss or self-consciousness, knelt down on the pavement and pressed their foreheads to the ground. Robert and Hubert thought it was very funny. They began pointing and laughing. Christian didn't laugh, but he was puzzled. "Mummy, what are they doing?"

"They're praying to God." Now all three were looking confused. She repeated calmly, "They're saying their prayers. You mustn't make fun of them. They worship God, just like us." But, insisted Christian, was it the *same* God? Yes, the same God.

Christian was five, going on six. Robert, the eldest, was seven and Hubert four. Two smaller children were waiting for them at home: two-year-old Henry, and baby Ghislaine who was the only girl so far. The small garrison town of Maison-Carrée, where their parents Guy and Monique de Chergé had brought them to live, was about 10 km from Algiers. Shortly after this incident Monique treated the older boys to a trip into the city, took them into its great Catholic basilica, and pointed out to them the inscription above the image of Mary. Christian was doing well with his reading and hardly needed any help to work it out: "Our Lady of Africa pray for us and for the Muslims".

Monique was a great believer in prayer. Every day she set time aside to pray and read the Scriptures. God alone knew how much the world needed his salvation at this terrible time! And surely it was a special providence for their family that had brought about Guy's sudden promotion to command of a regiment in Algeria. At the time it had seemed a routine posting. They had taken ship in October 1942, delighted to leave behind the greyness, food shortages and political uncertainty of life in Nîmes under the Vichy regime. But hardly had they settled into the officers' quarters at Maison-Carrée before Montgomery's victory at El Alamein in Egypt was followed up by the Allied landings in Algeria and Morocco. The Nazis reacted by promptly occupying the whole of France - but the French territories in Africa went over to the Allies, with General Charles de Gaulle of the Free French formally assuming power in Algeria.

In November 1943 Guy de Chergé crossed back over the sea with his regiment to join the Allied invasion of Italy. His children left behind at Maison-Carrée were sad that Daddy had to be away so often, but the war itself wasn't an everyday reality as it was for so many children in Europe. The next three years were a golden time, passed almost entirely in the peace and safety of the officers' quarters. When they went out into the town, to Mass or catechism classes, or for an excursion with Mummy, Christian enjoyed watching the two different worlds which co-existed here in Algeria: the French one with its neat shops, streets and parks, and the Arab one which was so excitingly different. He particularly liked going out on Fridays, because Friday was the big market day when the country people arrived from all around bringing sheep for sale, and also the day when huge crowds gathered to pray in the mosques. But he couldn't help noticing how the two worlds had hardly anything to do with each other. He never saw French and Algerian children playing together, or even coming out of the same schools. When he and Robert went off to summer camp there were no Muslim boys there: the

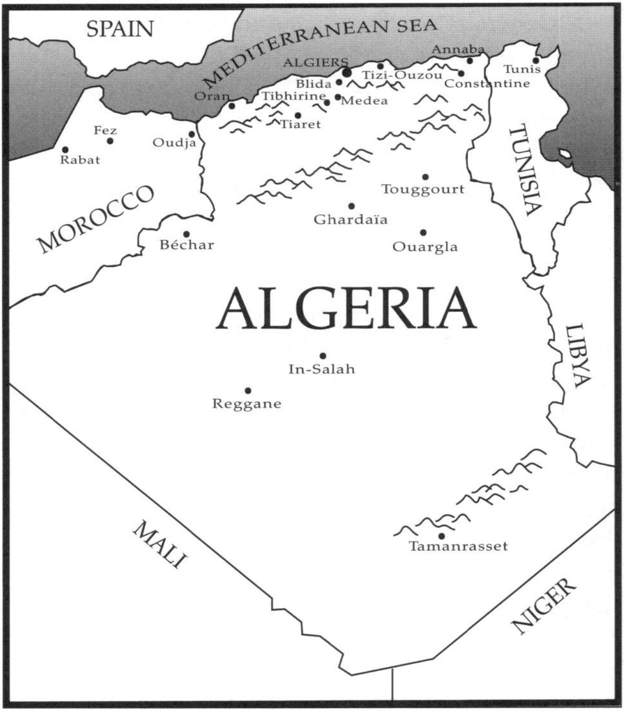

Map adapted from cover of *L'Algérie Devant Dieu* by Christian de Chergé.

camp was strictly reserved for the sons of French army officers and civil servants.

The French in Algeria

Over a hundred years before, in June 1830, a French fleet had suddenly appeared off the Algerian coast. The army sent to oppose it was routed in a pitched battle on the plateau of Staouëli, and on 5th July apparently generous surrender terms were agreed, guaranteeing free exercise of the Islamic religion and respect for the persons and property of the Algerian people. No sooner were they signed, however, than the French troops ran amok in Algiers, stealing everything they could lay their hands on. Over the next few years, while the invaders consolidated their hold over the areas immediately surrounding Algiers and other ports along the coast, many houses and other buildings - including mosques - were arbitrarily seized. Some were commandeered by the army, others quietly reassigned to prospective colonists coming over from Europe to settle in Algeria and make their fortunes. A bishop was appointed for Algiers, a network of parishes established for the new European settlements, and religious orders invited to come over to provide social services. In 1843, at the explicit request of the Governor General, Thomas Bugeaud, a Trappist monastery was founded at Staouëli. So keen was Bugeaud to obtain monks there that he made available over 1,000 hectares of land, and a money grant of 60,000 francs. The land was a mixture of sand dunes and malarial swamps, but the Trappists - like the monastic communities of mediaeval Europe - were to turn it into a model farm to serve as a beacon of agricultural excellence.

Muslim resistance

An *emir* (leader) emerged to mobilise Muslim resistance: Abdelkader, son of the hereditary head of Algeria's largest sufi brotherhood. Sufism, a mystical and esoteric form of Islam, had always been looked on with suspicion by mainstream Muslim theologians, but it was far and away the most important spiritual and social force in rural Algeria. As yet less than a tenth of the country was effectively under French control: Abdelkader rapidly established dominion over most of the vast interior, and large parts of the coast too. His writ ran even in the city of Medea, only about 60 km from Algiers. No religious bigot, he responded chivalrously to an appeal by the bishop of Algiers, Antoine Dupuch, for the exchange of prisoners. He would have done a deal with the French, letting them keep some small coastal enclaves if they would only leave him to rule the rest of the country in peace, but this possible compromise was rejected. Bugeaud adopted a ruthless policy of laying waste the countryside to prevent any supplies reaching the enemy. By December 1847 the Algerians were facing starvation.

Abdelkader had never desired power for its own sake. He had believed it was God's will for him to fight; now it was clear there was no chance of success, it must be God's will that he should stop fighting. To save his people further suffering, he surrendered in return for a promise to be allowed to go into exile in the Middle East. This promise was not honoured; he and his household were taken to Europe and imprisoned for five years, but eventually he was permitted to settle in Damascus. He lived there quietly for the rest of his life, spending his time in theological reflection and teaching, prayer and meditation, and writing poetry. Although he naturally had a large question mark about the behaviour of the supposedly Christian French towards him, he never allowed it to embitter his soul. When religious riots broke out in Damascus in 1860 and local Muslims began massacring the Syrian Christians and the European residents, he sheltered over a thousand people in his house and, by organising his own entourage and the city's other Algerian residents to defend the Christian quarter, saved at least another 10,000 lives there.

Annexation and occupation

Algeria was desperately poor and underdeveloped. Believing that only Europeans would know how to develop it properly, the French launched an enthusiastic advertising campaign to encourage more settlers. They even passed a decree making Algeria part of France - a sort of off-shore annexe. Huge tracts of the best agricultural land were confiscated and parceled out to the settlers, but very few of them made a success of farming. The vast majority settled in the towns and found work in the service sector, the hopes of economic prosperity with which they had crossed the Mediterranean largely disappointed. Although they might enjoy excellent public amenities in the French-style towns, many of them were miserably poor. Yet however poor they were, as French citizens with full civil rights they could always pride themselves on being a cut above the Arabs. In principle, should any Muslim choose to adopt a thoroughly French lifestyle he could apply for citizenship, but only if he was willing to renounce his Muslim civil status; since this was seen as a form of apostasy, virtually nobody was ever prepared to do it. That suited the settlers fine: it legitimated the perpetuation of a system of institutionalised inequality under which Muslim Algerians were discriminated against, exploited and taxed for the benefit of the French ascendancy, which would make sure to keep things that way for over a century.

Muslim tolerance, republican persecution

The missionary priests and Sisters who set up schools and clinics in Muslim villages took it for granted that the right way ahead for the Algerians was gradually to adopt the French language and culture, and its values - with the

Christian faith as part of the package. Such a process, they assumed, would proceed naturally so long as the Muslims were treated kindly, and nothing was done to upset them or rush them into things they weren't yet ready for. Only with the elapse of time did it become clear that they were not prepared to sacrifice their religion or their distinct identity as a people. Nevertheless they appreciated the sincere goodwill of the missionaries and the practical assistance they gave, and treated with courtesy and respect any Christians whom they saw taking their own faith seriously. They were deeply shocked to see how few did. Most settlers were nominally Catholic, but as the nineteenth century wore on their society - like that of France itself - came to be dominated by republicans espousing a deep and bitter anti-clericalism. Religious orders, in particular, aroused their hatred and suspicion. A law of Napoleon's time declaring them illegal had never been repealed, and in 1880 the government began to score cheap political points by enforcing it selectively.

From Staouëli to Tibhirine

Staouëli weathered this initial storm, and continued to prosper. Even the irreligious were generally prepared to acknowledge that its presence in Algeria was 'useful'. From it were founded churches and schools in all the villages round about, and relief measures were organised in times of famine. Its wine label, 'Domaine de la Trappe', was justly famous. Over the years a steady stream of new monks came out from France, mostly from Staouëli's mother-house, Aiguebelle, and a few were recruited from among the local settlers. At its peak it had the status of an abbey, with a hundred monks, and an even larger number of paid employees earning their living in its fields and workshops. Yet the threat hanging over the religious orders persisted. Most of them were finding it advisable to set up houses outside French territory, so they would have somewhere to go if, or when, the crunch came: among the many foreign foundations instituted for this reason was a Trappist monastery in Slovenia. Following another anti-clerical crackdown just after the turn of the century, the abbot of Staouëli decided to get out while the going was good: in 1904 the flourishing farm with its famous vineyards was sold, and the monks transferred to Italy.

Our Lady of Atlas

Paradoxically, on the eve of the Second World War the position of the Slovenian house became in turn frighteningly insecure, and its community sought the help of Aiguebelle to relocate once again - to Algeria. There was no question of being able to recover Staouëli. Eventually the monks identified a country estate, with a large mansion, established by English settlers in the nineteenth century 7 km from Medea. High up in the Atlas Mountains, the property comprised 374 hectares; its name 'Tibhirine' was Berber for

'The Gardens'. The hill on which it stood commanded a superb view of the surrounding countryside: it was one of the vantage points from which Abdelkader had directed his troops against the French. In 1939 the monks retrieved from Staouëli a large statue of the Virgin Mary, brought it to Tibhirine and installed it on a prominence known as Abdelkader's Rock from where it gazed out in blessing over the neighbourhood: Our Lady of Atlas.

1944 - France is liberated, not Algeria

On 6th June 1944 the Allies landed in Normandy, and in August Paris was liberated. Early the following year, Christian's father was able to be at home for his eighth birthday. The day before, a very special present had arrived: a second baby sister who was baptised Claire. Almost immediately afterwards Guy had to leave again - but by now it was clear that Hitler was finished, and indeed Germany surrendered in May 1945. Yet for the Algerians there was a painful irony in the VE celebrations: what about the liberation of their own people?

Christian grows up in France

Monique and the children were no longer in Algeria. They were flown back to France in the bomb bay of a military aircraft - not a comfortable ride, but an unforgettable thrill for the boys! Christian acquired two more little brothers during the post-war years: Jacques, and Gérard to whom he stood godfather. His teen years, like his earlier childhood, were spent in a sheltered and socially privileged environment. He attended a private Catholic secondary school, and in his leisure time was heavily involved with the Scout Movement. At seventeen he informed his parents that he'd decided to train for the priesthood. They weren't the least bit surprised. Monique was delighted. As for Guy, he wasn't opposed to the idea, but he was anxious to be sure the boy didn't rush into anything before he was really old enough to make up his own mind. He insisted firmly that Christian go to university first and see a bit of the wider world. Christian met this condition by enrolling for a one-year foundation course at the Sorbonne.

Thinking about being a priest

His free time was still largely devoted to scouting activities, now with an older group of Rover Scouts. Together they climbed up Mont Blanc, explored the Scriptures, and sought to engage with the problems of underprivileged groups in French society. On Thursday afternoons Christian helped out with a children's club in a working-class parish, and on Sundays with a scheme to build homes for poor families. At Eastertime the Rovers conducted 'missions' to de-christianised villages, helping the parish priest to put on special events and implement liturgical renewal. Years later, one of them reflected philosophically that it might not have converted the villagers, but it certainly converted some of them! Out of this group of around thirty lads, nine went on to become priests.

War of Independence

Whereas the dismantling of Britain's colonial empire had begun soon after the ending of the Second World War, the French were determined to hang on to theirs. Immediately they were plunged into unwinnable conflicts across the globe. Defeat in Vietnam in 1954 was followed by a fresh flare-up in Algeria when a new revolutionary movement - the Front de Libération Nationale (FLN) - issued a stirring call for independence. The French authorities massively overreacted, arresting people indiscriminately, and punishing whole communities for incidents whenever the real culprit couldn't be identified. To deny the FLN any potential support base, hundreds of thousands of Algerian peasants were forcibly 'regrouped' away from their homes and farms into secure zones where they could be both protected and closely supervised.

Seminary and military service

Faced simultaneously with revolt in Tunisia and Morocco, France quickly cut its losses by conceding independence to those colonies. But the 1,200,000-strong Algerian settler population maintained a very active political lobby in Paris, reminding everyone that *Algeria* was supposed to be an integral part of France: to give up part of France was unthinkable. In the short term, military repression proved remarkably effective: the FLN guerillas fled across the Tunisian border and a 200km long electrified fence, the Morice Line, was erected to prevent them from coming back. But could that level of repression be kept up indefinitely, while the grievances which had given rise to the insurgency continued to be ignored? A reform package was announced, but it wasn't anything like good enough: the settlers were determined to block any real change.

Terrorism condemned

Very early on in the campaign against the FLN, the army chaplaincy service passed word to the Archbishop of Algiers, Léon-Étienne Duval, that suspects were being tortured. He immediately issued a pastoral letter reminding everyone of Pope Pius XII's condemnation of the use of torture. As the conflict wore on, and hardliners on both sides persisted in responding to acts of terrorism with equally terrorist 'reprisals', he fearlessly denounced all acts of violence against the innocent regardless of who committed them. In the Arab districts and in the mountains the Muslims liked to listen to him on the radio, because he stood up for what was good and right, and gave them hope. The settlers, furious at his refusal to support 'his own people' regardless of moral considerations, dubbed him 'Mohammed Duval'.

Christian began studying for the priesthood in October 1956 at the Carmes, the most intellectually demanding of the Paris diocesan seminaries. He was 19. All the seminarians knew that after completing the initial two-year philosophy course, they would be called up to do their military service, and that meant being sent to Algeria. Christian's father was already out there (in 1957 he won his general's stars), and in August 1958 his brother Robert was posted to Souk-Ahras on the Tunisian border, to help patrol and maintain the Morice Line. In September that year Christian reported for duty and commenced officer training, at the end of which he was commissioned as a sub-lieutenant.

Monks at Tibhirine

Soon after the Second World War a wave of fresh recruits had entered Our Lady of Atlas, Tibhirine. The number of monks quickly rose to 35, and the house was given abbey status. Among the recent arrivals was a young Algerian-born settler, Amédée Noto. Luc Dochier, a transferee from Aiguebelle, was something of an oddity: a qualified medical doctor, he had insisted on entering as a lay brother, though it was virtually de rigueur for someone with a good education to become a choir monk and be ordained to the priesthood. The humbleness of lay brother status seemed important to him, but also the comparative freedom which it gave: lay brothers weren't obliged to spend hours and hours in chapel, and this left Luc free to do what he really liked doing - which was helping the long lines of people who began coming to the monastery each day from the villages round about, asking the see the *toubib* (doctor). In principle lay brothers did not participate in chapter meetings, but it became the practice to invite Luc because his opinion was so highly valued; he agreed to attend "out of obedience".

During the War of Independence there was considerable guerrilla activity in the mountains round about. The monks often heard gunfire or the noise of military planes flying overhead, and other European-owned estates were attacked, but the monastery was never touched. The guerrillas didn't see the monks as enemies, and knew the *toubib* provided medical services for the neighbouring villages. Luc was often called on to treat soldiers fighting on the French side, but he also responded to appeals for help from the FLN. In 1958 some families from Tamesguida, the nearest village which lay a few kilometres below in the valley, fled up the mountain and settled in the oasis of peace surrounding the monastery. They never returned to Tamesguida but formed a new small village close by, known as Tibhirine after the Trappist estate. The monks started a little primary school for their children.

Monks taken hostage

The only incident involving the monastery occurred one summer evening in 1959. Just as the bell rang for Compline, an FLN unit appeared in the courtyard. The commandant explained that he had been ordered to take two monks hostage: it was an act of reprisal because an *imam* (prayer leader) in Medea had been arrested for preaching politicised sermons, and "shot while trying to escape". He was polite and quite embarrassed by his mission, but pointed out that if he didn't obey his orders he himself would be shot, and someone less sympathetic would be sent to do the job. The abbot called the monks together to discuss what to do. Mathieu, an Italian whose sympathies were solidly on the side of the insurgents, immediately volunteered to go. When Luc arrived on the scene he shrugged and said they could take him, too. For two weeks the monks had to travel with the guerillas through the mountains, marching long distances over rough country each night, and hiding up during the day. Luc's asthma began playing him up terribly. One day a new recruit joined the group and was shocked to recognise Luc. "Are you crazy, holding him prisoner?" he demanded of the others. "This is the *toubib* - he looked after us for free!" The revelation was decisive: the commander took the two monks to the main road, issued them each with a bus ticket and left them free to make their way home. But by then Luc was so ill he had to be repatriated to France for medical treatment.

Christian's military posting

Sub-Lieutenant Christian de Chergé was posted to Tiaret, a small market town in the Atlas Mountains 300 km west of Algiers. On 19th July 1959 he took up his duties in a village to the north of the town named Aïn Said. General de Chergé had pulled strings to ensure that his pacifically-minded seminarian son could do his military service with a unit of the Specialised Administrative Sections (SAS), which had been set up to win hearts and minds by genuinely improving the quality of life of the rural majority. SAS fieldworkers lived out in the countryside in order to get to know the Muslim villagers, help them to adopt modern agricultural techniques and form co-operatives, and ensure smooth running of key social services like schools and clinics. Only a relatively small aspect of Christian's duties while he was in Aïn Said was strictly military: he was in charge of a *maghzen*, a unit of thirty Muslim home guardsmen which periodically patrolled the surrounding countryside to interdict guerilla activity.

Christian and Mohammed

The sunshine and mountain scenery brought back all his old magical childhood feelings about Algeria, and he was delighted at the opportunities his posting would give him to get to know ordinary Muslims. Over the next month a friendship developed between him and a village policeman named Mohammed. It was an unlikely relationship, given that they were so widely apart in age and experience. Mohammed was an older married man with ten children and, although like so many Algerians of his generation he had picked up spoken French, he had had no formal schooling and had known poverty all his life. Christian, the privileged intellectual, was a very *young* 22. What attracted him to Mohammed was his deep spirituality born out of a life of faithful prayer. He didn't talk much, but what he said made sense, and he was a good listener. Here was someone Christian could talk to about his own life with God, and be understood. Mohammed also responded with ready understanding to Christian's ambivalence about the war and its politics; it struck a chord in the ambivalence of his own position, as an Algerian Muslim working for the French state. To the FLN he was a collaborator and a traitor. He knew that, and yet he didn't hate the FLN; he understood their point of view, too...

Aïn Said was normally very peaceful, but the guerrillas could suddenly appear anywhere, any time. One day when Christian and Mohammed happened to be taking a walk together, they ran into trouble. Christian was very struck by the way Mohammed handled the incident: intervening first to protect Christian, then to defuse the situation and discourage reprisals against the guerrillas. Once all was quiet again, Christian did what he could - which wasn't much - to organise some additional protection for Mohammed over the next few days: they both knew that his actions had made him a target for assassination. Before they parted Christian added, "I'll pray for you."

"I know you'll pray for me," quietly replied Mohammed. "But you see, Christians don't know how to pray!" A few days later he was found dead near one of the village wells, his throat cut.

Referendum and Algerian independence

As an officer Christian had been placed in Aïn Said only briefly, to gain some hands-on knowledge of how the SAS worked on the ground. On 1st September he returned to Tiaret, to work in an office co-ordinating the efforts of the fieldworkers in the surrounding countryside. The whole area was relatively peaceful, and the remainder of his war uneventful. The chaplaincy service was an important source of moral support, as were army friendships with Catholics who, like himself, were both solid in their faith and deeply concerned about the justice issues raised by the counter-insurgency. Mgr Duval appeared to him as a light shining in the darkness, and it was a memorable day for him when, during a retreat in Algiers for seminarian conscripts, he had the chance to meet the outspoken archbishop for the first time in person. Meanwhile the number of military servicemen being killed or maimed, and the revulsion expressed by many of those who returned home at some of the things they had been expected to take part in, were swinging French opinion against the war. Even General de Gaulle began speaking of an 'Algerian Algeria', under its own government and laws, and in January 1961 a referendum resulted in a massive 'yes' in favour of self-determination.

Study for the priesthood

Christian's military service had ended at the beginning of that year. He went straight back to Paris and plunged again into his studies. He didn't talk much about his experiences, and said nothing to anyone about what had happened in Aïn Said, but Algeria had made a huge impact on him: those who knew him agreed that he'd gone out still a kid, and come back a man. Meanwhile, outraged by de Gaulle's 'betrayal', settlers and disgruntled army professionals turned to extremist right-wing movements - and overwhelmingly to the nastiest and bloodiest of them all, the OAS (Organisation Armée Secrète). In March 1962 an agreement was reached at Evian between the French government and the FLN, and the last few months of the transition to independence began. The OAS plunged into a final orgy of fanatical violence, sabotaging industrial installations, burning the university library in Algiers, assassinating any settler or French official who hadn't supported them, and killing Muslims at random. Evian had in fact won a reasonably good deal for the settlers in an independent Algeria, and the new government had no wish to lose these people whose education, skills and liquid capital could help in the task of building a new nation. But they weren't interested. Already they were heading en masse over to Europe: over a million men, women and children left Algeria before the end of the year.

Most of the Catholic clergy left along with the settlers. The few who remained needed to be willing to accept the catastrophic reversal of living in an independent Algeria, in which Islam would be the national religion. The bishops, and some of the priests and religious who chose to stay, took Algerian citizenship. Virtually all the church buildings had become redundant, and were turned into mosques or community centers, leaving to Christian use just the few that were still really needed: the European - nominally Christian - population of Algeria had already fallen to 100,000, and practising Catholics numbered only a few thousand. Christian clergy, like the *imams* who served the mosques, would from now on receive their salaries from the Muslim state.

Members of nursing and teaching congregations often stayed, knowing that their work would be needed and valued all the more in the new Algeria. But the Trappists at Tibhirine could see no future there for a contemplative monastery: virtually the whole community, including the abbot, returned to France, and the four monks who remained assumed it was only a matter of time before they would have to follow. However towards the end of that year Mgr Duval had a meeting with the former guerrilla leader who was now the *wali* (head of local government) for Medea and its surrounding district. It was the *wali* who raised the subject of the abbey: "Not far from here, in the mountains, there is a house of monks.

During the war they cared for our sick and wounded. I presume you won't disturb them."

To close or not to close Tibhirine

The archbishop certainly had no wish to disturb the monks: he wanted very much for them to stay. But Gabriel Sortais, Abbot General of the Cistercian Order of the Strict Observance - as the Trappists are officially called - disagreed. In November 1963 he drew up an order to close Our Lady of Atlas. Sortais and Duval were both in Rome for the Vatican Council, and Duval tried without success to persuade him to change his mind; the two had an angry row. That night Dom Gabriel suffered a massive heart attack and died. Tibhirine was reprieved - but for how long?

The abbot of Aiguebelle was elected to replace Sortais and a new abbot - Jean de la Croix - took over Aiguebelle. One of the priority tasks he set himself was to investigate personally the pros and cons of trying to preserve the Algerian house. He flew over to Algiers in February 1964, having arranged to stay with a priest-friend there. Fr Joseph Carmona was overjoyed to see him; he desperately needed to talk. Since independence all his parishioners had disappeared. The only thing that was keeping him going was being able to make retreats from time to time at Tibhirine, and he pleaded with the abbot to spare the monastery. Dom Jean next went to see Archbishop Duval who received him frostily, expecting yet another row, but his attitude soon changed: "You say the monks can stay? Well then, if the monks stay, the Church will live on!" The two were able to talk further in the car driving up to Tibhirine, and the abbot ended up totally convinced, assuring Duval that it would be better to close one of the large French abbeys than to close Atlas.

Two of those large French abbeys - Aiguebelle itself, and Timadeuc - each sent four monks that year, offering some hope for the future although, inevitably, the new arrivals would need to go through a careful process of discernment to discover whether their future really did lie in Algeria. Two of them certainly settled in well - tough little Jean-Pierre Schumacher from Alsace, and Aubin who had previously been a White Father and already spoke fluent Arabic. Because Aubin taught in the school he was addressed as 'Sheikh' by the village children, as was Amédée who sometimes helped out with classes. Another reinforcement who had no problem acclimatising was Luc, the *toubib*, who now happily returned to Algeria. On Mgr Duval's advice, the monastery handed over most of its land to the state, retaining only 14 hectares - as much as they could cultivate, and enough to maintain their small community. Besides a vegetable garden and orchard where they grew most of their own food, the remnant of their estate included a small vineyard, olive trees and an oil press. A plot was set aside for growing lavender, which was dried for sale, but the main cash income came from the beehives, which each year produced over 400 k of the superb honey which connoisseurs called 'Trappist Gold'.

In a surprise move in 1965 Mgr Duval - primate of one of the world's tiniest and least powerful Churches - was made a cardinal. Pope Paul VI, at least, seemed to agree that the ongoing Christian presence in Algeria had something important to say to the modern world.

PRIEST IN FRANCE - MONK IN ALGERIA

On 21st March 1964 Christian was ordained to the priesthood in the historic church of St Sulpice in Paris, and in June he was given his first posting: to the Basilica of the Sacré Coeur, Montmartre. It wasn't easy for him to accept this assignment. He was already quite sure that he was called not to parish ministry but to the monastic life - and also that God wanted him to go back to North Africa, to live a life of prayer *there* - but he had been asked first to give five years to the Diocese of Paris. Longing for a life of apostolic simplicity and solidarity with the poor, Christian could never feel at home in the magnificent but tasteless basilica, helping with pastoral programmes which he saw as old-fashioned and triumphalistic. Nevertheless for exactly five years he patiently and conscientiously put up with it. The post had its compensations, one of which was acting as headmaster of the choir school. *That* he managed very well: he knew how to bring out the best in young people, and they both respected and liked him. He didn't complain - at least, not too openly or loudly - and given his background he seemed to fit beautifully into the set-up on Montmartre: people were sure he'd found his niche. Everyone was astonished when at the end of June 1969 he suddenly cleared out his office, gave away most of his books, and announced, "I'm off to Algeria. I'm going to become a Trappist monk so I can go and pray with the Muslims."

To Atlas - via Aiguebelle

The process of joining the Cistercian Order starts with entering a particular community to follow a novitiate, leading up to profession - and profession includes a vow of *stability*, a commitment to remain always in that community. A monk *may* transfer elsewhere, but he won't do it lightly, and it's not purely his personal decision but requires a process of discernment involving the whole community. Quietly and discreetly, while he was at Montmartre, Christian had been gathering information, and when he put in his application he made it clear straightaway that he was asking for something exceptional - something which involved a bending of the normal rules. He wanted to become a monk at Our Lady of Atlas, Tibhirine. But since he couldn't do a novitiate there - because the community wasn't large enough - he was applying to enter the mother-house, Aiguebelle, on the understanding that his eventual vow of stability would be to Atlas. This was somewhat irregular. More crucially, at that time it was considered unwise for *anybody* to be permitted to take a vow of stability in Algeria, since the future of the community there appeared so uncertain. However the Abbot of Aiguebelle was Jean de la Croix, one of Atlas' most determined allies. He agreed to the terms laid down.

Having duly completed a period of novitiate, Christian arrived back once again in Algeria on 15th January 1971, a few days before his 34th birthday which he would celebrate at Tibhirine. He had never before seen the house and community to which he was determined to commit himself for the rest of his life. Some aspects disappointed him. The premises were grander than he'd expected - ridiculously large for the handful of monks rattling around inside - and although they weren't luxurious their size seemed to evoke the painful inequalities of the colonial past. Although this bothered him, it didn't seem to bother the local Muslims whom he described admiringly as: "poor but smiling, proud and without resentment, believers, and respectful towards a monk whoever he may be - so long as what's in the back of the shop matches the window display." Eager to prepare himself for a future in which he was sure, under God's leading, his destiny would be linked to theirs, he threw himself into learning Arabic: both the dialect spoken by 99% of the population, and classical Arabic which was now, in its modern literary form, the country's official language. Although the two forms were linked, they were so different that an older Algerian was more likely to understand French than literary Arabic.

Temporary vows

Studies had to be fitted in as and when, for the monastery was not an academic ivory tower. In addition to the long hours in chapel, praying the seven Hours of the Divine Office - Vigils at 4.00 am, Lauds at 7.30, Terce at 9.15, Sext at 12.30, None at 2.45, Vespers at 6.00 and Compline at 8.00 - there was plenty of hard manual labour to be got through. Christian didn't have a problem with these demands: he understood his own personality well enough to see that they were necessary for him, and were part of what seemed to be God's plan for his life, slowly and gradually unfolding before him. On 1st October 1971 he made his first, temporary vows. He had specially chosen the feastday of St Thérèse of Lisieux, the Carmelite whose hidden life turned out to have such an important message for today's world.

The community was a complete ragbag of men who'd come to Algeria for all sorts of reasons: some of them were oddballs by any standards, and Christian made yet another oddball to add to the collection. His arrival had brought the number of monks up to eleven, but only four were 'stabilised' in Atlas. The rest were on loan from other monasteries: they had the option of eventually deciding to transfer there permanently, but unless and until they came to that decision there was always a question mark about how long they would stay. A firm but discerning superior should have been able to bind them together with a sense of common purpose. But none of them were leadership material, and there weren't enough stabilised monks to hold a valid election. A series of *ad nutum* superiors were appointed by Aiguebelle, seconded from other monasteries and coming and going in rapid succession, each one taking a different line from his predecessor. The life of the monastery preserved a certain outward serenity thanks to the constant daily round of prayer and manual labour, and the persistent Trappist habit of eschewing unnecessary chatter. Underneath, the situation was a mess.

Friction in the community

From the start there was friction between Christian and the others. As a group they were quite elderly and he was the only one under 45, but it wasn't just a question of age. Between him and them loomed the massive watershed of the 1960s: Vatican II and Algerian independence. The older monks deserved every credit for the big effort they had made to adjust to the changes, but it hadn't been easy for them - whereas Christian, whose priestly formation had coincided with those changes, was completely at home with them and eager to move on still further into the unknown. The fact that intellectually, he had the edge on everyone else didn't make him any more popular. Nor did the pig-headedness with which he sometimes insisted on defending his point of view. The older monks did their best to swallow their irritation while they waited patiently for him to realise that he'd mistaken his vocation. If he was so keen to work with the Muslims he'd do better to transfer as a secular priest to the Diocese of Algiers, or perhaps join the Little Brothers of Jesus.

Roman interlude

In August 1972 Jean de la Croix intervened to give both sides a break, sending Christian off to do a two-year course in Arabic and Islamology at the Pontifical Institute of Arab Studies in Rome. He came back more convinced than ever of being called to spend his life "praying with the Muslims". To his delight he was now put in charge of the guesthouse. Practising Christians in Algeria were few and scattered, but for the most part they were people to whom their faith was vital: clergy, religious and committed laypeople pondering on how to be Church in an Islamic environment, aid workers, technological advisers and students from all over the world. All these people came to the monastery from time to time - some for organised retreats and meetings, others as individuals or as groups of friends visiting on a casual basis. Christian hung an additional notice on the door: "MUSLIMS ARE WELCOME TO MAKE RETREATS HERE". For several years in succession he renewed his vows, but still on a temporary basis. Meanwhile, in the eyes of his confreres, the eccentricity of his behaviour increased. He fasted throughout Ramadan, slipped his sandals off before entering the chapel, and took to greeting everyone in Arab fashion. That he quite often took short breaks away from the monastery, in response to invitations from the diocese or other religious communities to give talks or retreats, provided a safety valve - but it also underlined the distance between Christian and the rest of the community.

Solemn Profession

Jean de la Croix continued to hope and pray that the struggling daughter-house in Algeria would survive and flourish. During a visit in autumn 1976 he spoke to each of the monks individually. This had to be their choice: there was no point in his trying to push them, but the fact that *he* believed in the future of the foundation would be a major factor in each man's process of discernment. Christian, given the opportunity to explain before all the brothers how he understood his own vocation, for the first time told them about Mohammed in Aïn Said, describing how the self-sacrificing death of this Muslim friend had led him to the conviction that God was calling him to live a life of prayer in Algeria, not alone but in a community "in order to be truly a witness of the Church". Our Lady of Atlas was his "chosen fiancée". Like any other fiancée this community wasn't perfect in the way he'd imagined, but in its unique reality he would encounter God in encountering the other. There ensued a miracle of communion: it was agreed that he should make his solemn profession, and four other brothers decided to be stabilised at Atlas. Christian chose once again the date of 1st October. After the ceremony he asked forgiveness of the community for the many times he had behaved insensitively.

Potential new recruits continued to arrive from time to time, but almost always left again. The most promising was Christophe Lebreton. Christophe had lost his faith while in junior seminary and gone on to university to study law. When the big student riots broke out in 1968 he was on the streets, shouting and protesting with the rest, when suddenly he asked himself what good he thought this was going to achieve. Abruptly losing his faith in left-wing politics as well, he began spending the summer holidays as a volunteer with the Abbé Pierre's Emmaus movement. Working with the homeless, he became convinced that the way to find God was through being close to the poor. Called up for national service, Christophe opted to serve his time doing voluntary work in Algeria; teaching in an Algiers school and helping with a centre for disabled children. One day Fr Carmona took him to Mass at Tibhirine, where he immediately fell in love with the idea of monastic life. Back in France he entered the Trappist Abbey of Tamié, but soon began acting up when he found it too luxurious and formal for his taste. The abbot sent him to see a psychiatrist, but the psychiatrist reported that there was nothing wrong with Christophe; perhaps there was

The Brothers, from left to right: Jean-Pierre, Paul, Amédée, Luc, Michel, Philippe, Christophe and Christian. At the monastery of Our Lady of Atlas, 1994.

something wrong with the monastery? He had never forgotten Our Lady of Atlas, and applied to be transferred there in 1975. It was at Atlas that he took his temporary vows the following December, when he was still only 26. Sadly, he then got cold feet. It was partly due to personality clashes with Christian - although, or perhaps because, they were so alike. Relating to such an elderly community was also a major problem for him, and he returned to France. The experience must have done him some good, since now he managed to settle down happily at Tamié.

Ribat - Catholics and Islam

In 1979 some Catholics who were living and working in Algeria, and who were interested in exploring the spiritual world of Islam, formed a group to meet regularly for discussion. They took the name 'Ribat-es-Salam', which meant literally 'Bond of Peace' and was partly an allusion to Ephesians 4:3. In Arabic 'ribat' also meant a fortified monastery of a type which, during the early years of the Islamic era, was often established near the frontiers between the shrinking Byzantine and expanding Arab empires, to function as a 'stronghold of prayer' but also as a military watchtower. The group hoped to become a 'stronghold of prayer' *without* the historical aspect of violence and hostility. Jean de la Croix encouraged the Ribat to meet at Tibhirine, in order to root its explorations in the monastic tradition, and Christian immediately became involved.

No one else in the community did. Some of them felt distinctly uncomfortable about this attempt to engage so directly with Islam as a religion. But mostly they just weren't interested in all the talk, talk, talk - which in any case they couldn't follow. Nobody except Christian had ever had the chance to undertake serious studies in Arabic and Islamology. Old Luc used to say that for him, reading the Koran was like reading a railway timetable. Christian, for his part, was unable as yet fully to appreciate the very warm way in which the other monks related to Muslims as *people*. Amédée for example, whom the impetuous Christian considered a diehard pre-Vatican II Cistercian traditionalist, was invited to all the local weddings and festivals. He was also the village scribe to whom the women came when they needed letters written to absent sons and daughters, and to whom they turned whenever they needed to have a good cry in sympathetic company.

The sufis of Medea

The previous Christmas a group of young Catholics from Madagascar, who were studying at Medea University, had turned up at the monastery - late - for midnight Mass. Jean-Pierre, who was in charge of the singing, noticed they had good voices, so in the lead-up to Christmas 1979 he went to Medea to practise them a bit beforehand - and remind them not to be late again! When he arrived at the centre where they were staying they were out, and he ended up chatting instead to the person in charge, a very pious Muslim and a member of a sufi brotherhood. This man asked if he, too, could come to the Christmas services. Shortly after Christmas he came again, bringing quite a large group of fellow-sufis, together with their wives, to visit the monastery. Although some of the monks were rather nervous about the idea, it was arranged for them to spend the Feast of Epiphany at Tibhirine, and for the chapel to be used throughout that day alternately for the Divine Office and the Muslim prayers. Over the next few years about a dozen of the sufis became involved in the Ribat, participating regularly in the three-day residential meetings which took place in spring and autumn each year. The Christian Ribat members, well aware of the traditional tension between sufism and mainstream Islam, welcomed the sufis' participation while at the same time making special efforts also to involve a few 'normal' Muslims for the sake of balance.

One day an Islamist student rent-a-mob suddenly arrived in Tibhirine to deface the statue of Our Lady of Atlas, leaving both arms broken off at the elbow and a deep gash in the belly. When the monks heard about it they were shocked and hurt. So were the local Muslims. For years the women from the villages round about had brought flowers to 'Lalla Mariam', the Virgin Mother of the Prophet Jesus honoured in the Koran, and prayed for her help. They made a garden round the desecrated statue to show how sad they were.

A prior for Atlas - Christian is chosen

On 11th May 1984 Aubin died. A large crowd turned up to see him laid to rest in the monastery garden alongside the graves of past monks: a small number of Christians and an overwhelming majority of Muslims. The community had never fully realised how much affection the neighbours had for 'Sheikh Aubin'. A particularly fond memory was of how, when he served as porter, he used to give drinks of water to anyone who called at the monastery gate. In North Africa, as in Palestine, the gift of a cup of cold water is deeply significant. Aubin's going to God brought the brothers closer to the villagers, and also closer to each other.

The time for the next General Chapter of the Cistercian Order was approaching, and Jean de la Croix was worried. If Atlas had still not regularised its situation this would perhaps lead to renewed talk of closure. By now nine monks were stabilised, with the right to vote. Unfortunately three were absent. This was usually the case at any time - especially since, given the age profile and small size of the community, and the harshness of its life, anyone who fell seriously ill had to be sent away to be properly looked after. Agreeing however that the urgency of the situation demanded it, the remaining six came together to hold the necessary deliberations and vote on the future of the community. Christian's proposal that the house adopt the status of autonomous priory - rather than that of abbey, which suggested something on a much grander scale than

Tibhirine - was accepted. The monks then proceeded to hold an election for prior, and the choice fell on Christian.

The prior-elect had to set off fairly soon afterwards for Holyoke in the USA to take his place at the General Chapter. The gathering seemed to him to be dominated by the abbots of large and important monasteries from the rich, developed world - a whole monastic scene, complete with grandiose ceremonial, which he saw as of the past rather than of the future. Himself he saw as representing the voices of Vatican II and of the Third World. The older abbots were perhaps somewhat surprised when he read out a fraternal message from the sufis of Medea, but they happily gave him one to take back. A key point on his personal agenda was to obtain a small but significant amendment in the Order's constitution. Trappists were officially supposed to offer monastic hospitality to "those who share our faith"; he wanted this changed to "people of goodwill". While in Holyoke, Christian also issued an appeal for other monasteries to send monks to Atlas. The assembled abbots took note of this appeal, and did their best to encourage serious consideration within their home communities of the idea of transferring to Atlas.

Tensions and strains at Atlas

Unfortunately, welcoming men to Algeria was only the start: the next question was how to keep them there. Living in so small a community could be quite claustrophobic, exacerbating the effect of minor differences and personality clashes. One of the principle irritants remained Christian himself: patience was not his strongest card, and in his early years as prior his handling of personal relations could be quite insensitive. Another serious obstacle was the poverty of the house. Since Vatican II monastic life wasn't usually as austere as it had been in the past, but at Atlas it was austere out of sheer necessity - and some prospective recruits couldn't take it. As time went on a further cause of tension arose, again centring on Christian. This was the growing importance of his role vis-à-vis the wider Christian community in Algeria: he was constantly in demand as a speaker, retreat-giver and spiritual director. The monks often felt that all their prior's concern and attention - his love, if you like - were lavished on the Muslims, the secular clergy and nuns, and the people staying in the guesthouse, leaving nothing over for them. When the circumstances of a community give rise to such a perception, the question of whether or not it is valid is perhaps beside the point: valid or not, it hurts.

New arrivals

Despite all the problems, a few of the newcomers liked what they found in Tibhirine, managed to adjust, and stayed. Before entering Bellefontaine Abbey in 1980 Michel Fleury had belonged to the Prado community in Marseilles, where he served the poor while working part-time in a factory. He had been particularly moved by his contacts with the North African immigrants, who were even more underprivileged than other groups in the city. Intrigued by Brother Aubin's obituary notice, written by Christian and distributed to all the Cistercian monasteries, he transferred to Atlas in 1984 at the age of 40. Bruno Lemarchand, also from Bellefontaine, was 54 but he rarely talked about himself. The brothers knew he had been a headmaster but not that, like Christian, he was the son of an army officer; he had been born in Vietnam and spent his childhood in Algeria.

Célestin Ringeard had first come to Algeria as an army medic in 1957. One day after a skirmish near Oran, a badly-wounded young guerrilla was taken prisoner. The soldiers in Célestin's unit wanted to finish him off. Célestin said they would do that over his dead body. He sat up all night nursing the man, Sidi, and next day arranged for him to be taken to hospital. Later, as a priest serving a slum district of Nantes, Célestin was always available to anyone in need. One night he got a frantic phonecall from a young homosexual threatening suicide. He set out immediately, but as he reached the block the boy jumped out of the window, dying smashed on the pavement in front of him. The experience left Célestin traumatised, but determined to find a way of engaging on a deeper level with the mysteries of suffering and evil: this determination brought him to Bellefontaine. Some years later an Algerian lad arrived to see him, having been directed to the monastery by the bishop of Nantes after many weeks of searching. It was Sidi's son, come to study in France and charged by his father with the task of tracking down the man who had saved his life - to say thank you. Célestin was 53 when he arrived in Atlas in 1986. He made an odd sort of Trappist: a restless and chatty type who, in the mornings when he was supposed to be meditating on the Scriptures, used to go off for long walks instead - often finding someone to talk to on the way. Christian determinedly turned a blind eye, giving him the space he needed.

In 1987 there was great rejoicing when Christophe Lebreton decided again to volunteer for Atlas. This time it worked out. Christophe was put in charge of the farm, and a new co-operative arrangement was set up whereby the monks and four 'assistants' from among the village men shared both work and profits on an equal basis. Ali, who had spent forty years working for the monks, was succeeded by his nephew Mohammed, who besides being chief assistant was also the gatekeeper and watchman; he lived with his family on the premises, and liked to take part in Ribat meetings. Paul Favre-Miville, son of a village blacksmith in the mountains of Savoy, was a qualified plumber and central heating expert. He had done his military service in Blida, not far from Tibhirine in the Atlas Mountains. Returning home to France he didn't marry but continued to live with his parents, and became a model parishioner: never missing Mass, singing in the choir, giving generously of his time and money for any good cause. But he was searching for something more. In the seventies he intensified his search, making pilgrimages to Rome, Jerusalem and Tamanrasset (Tamanrasset was the very remote spot in the south of the Sahara Desert where Charles de Foucauld had lived as a hermit, and where he was killed). Eventually he entered the Trappist monastery of Tamié in Savoy, where he would not be too far from his beloved family. Fairly soon after completing his novitiate he decided to respond to the appeal for recruits for Atlas, only deferring his departure until after his father's death. He arrived in 1989, aged 50.

John Paul II visits Morocco

Meanwhile, in 1985, Morocco hosted a Papal visit during which John Paul II addressed a crowd of 80,000 young Muslims in a stadium in Casablanca: "I believe that we, Christians and Muslims, must recognise with joy the religious values that we have in common, and give thanks to God for them. Both of us believe in one God, the only God, who is all Justice and all Mercy; we believe in the importance of prayer, of fasting, of almsgiving, of repentance and of pardon; we believe that God will be a merciful God to us at the end of time, and we hope that after the resurrection he will be satisfied with us and we know that we will be satisfied with him. Loyalty demands also that we should recognise and respect our differences. Obviously the most fundamental is the view that we hold on the person and work of Jesus of Nazareth. You know that for the Christians, this Jesus causes them to enter into an intimate knowledge of the mystery of God and into a filial communion by his gifts, so that they recognise him and proclaim him Lord and Saviour. Those are important differences, which we can accept with humility and respect, in mutual tolerance: there is a mystery there on which, I am certain, God will one day enlighten us."

A new community in Fez, Morocco

The enthusiasm with which the Pope was received led to Tibhirine, in 1988, opening an annexe - an embryonic daughter-house - across the border in neighbouring Morocco. The tiny community was sorely stretched to spare even a few monks for a second house. However the Algerian government wanted Tibhirine limited to a maximum of thirteen monks, so a linked house in a neighbouring country offered the only potential for increasing the overall size of the community to a more viable figure. It also meant that potential recruits denied visas by the Algerian government did not have to be turned away, because it was a lot easier to get into Morocco. A suitable house - a former hotel with a large garden - was found in Fez. It would ordinarily have four monks permanently in residence, with Bruno in charge. Because of its urban setting it couldn't be agricultural: workshops were set up where the monks would earn their living making eucharistic hosts and jam. Christian organised a rotation schedule between Tibhirine and Fez to give the brothers in each house a change of scenery and companionship from time to time. They travelled back and forth by car along the mountain roads, and on the journey out from Tibhirine the car was always loaded up with fresh produce from the vegetable garden.

1990 - Christian continues as prior

Tibhirine's village school had been taken over by the government, and in 1988 a mother-and-child clinic which had been run on monastery premises also closed. Christian wasn't worried: social services did tremendous good, but he had never seen them as the raison d'être for the Christian presence in Algeria. The clinic had been held in a room adjoining the enclosure wall, and Christian now offered the village the use of this room as a mosque and koran school. Soon the muezzin's call to prayer could be heard mingling with the sound of the monastery bell.

Christophe, who had been one of twelve children, loved being with people and had formed warm relationships all over France and Algeria. At his ordination, celebrated in Tibhirine on 1st January 1990, the chapel was packed: 27 members of his family were present, and half the seats were filled with his Muslim guests. Later that year Christian was re-elected as prior of Atlas. His first term might well have been a trial to the community, but monks have their feet firmly on the ground: they know that nobody is perfect. The brothers appreciated that Christian had tremendously positive qualities - however much these positive qualities contributed to making him difficult to live at close quarters with! They also appreciated that it was only his vision, and his clarity about his calling to Atlas, which had kept their community in being. Finally, Christian was still the only realistic candidate for prior: if they were unable to accept him as he was, the house would probably have to close. Nevertheless, in confirming his mandate, the brothers asked him to pay more attention to them in future - and also to pay more attention to his own needs, and not work himself quite so hard.

TOWARDS THE END

The FLN had become the ruling party of Algeria, no other parties being permitted, but had failed to deliver satisfactory solutions to the country's deepseated problems. The economy was in a worse state than ever, and social tensions had long been simmering between the tiny privileged elite and the masses of the dispossessed. Particularly disaffected were the students: they knew that however well they did in their studies, they would end up unemployed or in dead-end jobs. Living conditions had deteriorated badly, and the creaking socialistic state distribution system couldn't even keep the shops stocked with basic commodities. In response to an outbreak of riots and protests, the regime announced some democratic reforms allowing other political parties to be formed. Algeria's first free municipal elections for 24 years were held in June 1990, but they were boycotted by most of the new parties. To the government's astonishment its own FLN did quite poorly, leaving the field clear for a coalition of Islamist groups known as the FIS (Front Islamique du Salut) to win a landslide victory in most of the large towns. The 1991 general elections saw an extremely low turnout, but of those who did vote, a high proportion voted FIS. The FIS did so well that it appeared likely they would romp home with the two-thirds majority which would entitle them to amend the constitution. At this point the military stepped in, annulled the elections and dissolved the FIS.

Their hopes from the democratic process dashed, many Islamists turned to armed violence. It wasn't difficult to recruit fighters in a country where so many young men could see no future for themselves. As frustrations mounted and new insurgent movements multiplied, any sense of coherent purpose was lost. Ethical inhibitions against deliberately harming women, children, the elderly, teachers and religious leaders were dropped: anyone might become a target at any time, because of something they had done or something they were thought to have done. A number of guerrilla movements formed, but the GIA (Groupe Islamique Armée) was the most savage and dangerous. It wasn't a unified organisation, but a network of small quasi-autonomous units scattered across the country. The local GIA *emirs* were in constant rivalry, occasionally even fighting each other. In the competition to emerge as more ruthless and effective killers than all the rest, some of them insisted that a young man wishing to join their unit had first to demonstrate his zeal by killing a member of his own family.

Christian's response

The area around Medea became a battleground between the guerrillas and the army. To stress his community's absolute non-violence and neutrality, Christian encouraged the monks to call the guerrillas 'brothers of the mountains' and the army 'brothers of the plain'. The 'brothers of the mountains' were quite often to be seen praying in the Tibhirine mosque, or queueing up to see Luc; the monks schooled themselves not to react. Yet they knew that six army medics found to have treated guerrillas had been executed, and their heads left in the market place in Medea as a public warning. One day when Luc accompanied Jean-Pierre on a shopping trip to the town, some children playing on the streets grabbed his beard and taunted him, "Aren't you afraid of losing your head, too?" Luc growled, "I don't care. They can have it."

Ultimatum - foreigners to leave Algeria

In October 1993 the GIA issued an ultimatum, ordering all foreigners to leave Algeria before the end of the following month. Some did get out, but the majority just took extra precautions. Christian was summoned to Medea by the *wali*, who tried to persuade him to accept an armed garrison for the monastery's protection. He refused, partly on principle, but also because a military presence would make the house a target. He agreed only to instruct Mohammed not to open the gate to anyone after 7.30 pm -

though there was no way to stop anyone climbing over the wall. That autumn's Ribat meeting had to be held without the sufis: for security reasons the *wali* had forbidden them to come any more. On 1st December Christian drove to Algiers and spent the night there. Amédée, returning from a trip to France, needed to be met at the airport the following morning. Alone in his room that evening, acutely conscious that the GIA ultimatum had just expired, he began to compose a letter as a 'last message' to his family and friends. Just in case...

Killing campaign against foreigners

The killings of foreigners began almost immediately: one here, one there. The biggest shock for the monks at Tibhirine came on 15th December, when they heard on the radio the news of a massacre which had taken place the night before at Tamesguida. The twelve victims were their friends the 'Yugos', a group of Croats contracted by the state hydroelectric company to build a reservoir. For several years running they had come to Tibhirine for midnight Mass, but this Christmas they had been hoping to spend at home with their families. Partly because of the GIA ultimatum, but also because of the fighting which had flared up in former Yugoslavia between the Croats and the Bosnian Muslims, arrangements were being made for their repatriation lest they became a target of the Islamist fanatics. They were watching telly in their common room when a horde of guerrillas arrived, marched them outside and cut their throats.

Christmas Eve 1993

Once again, Christian was summoned by the *wali*, who pleaded with him to accept a garrison. Again he refused. The *wali* offered to put the monks up in a hotel in town at government expense, and taxi them each day to and from the monastery. Alternatively they should all take a long holiday in France. Christian would agree only to bring forward the time at which the monastery closed each evening: Mohammed would be told not to allow anyone in after 5.30. As calmly as possible the monks discussed the situation, going over their reasons for staying. They agreed that in the event of an attack on the monastery, there should be no pointless heroics: each brother should do his best to flee or hide.

Christmas this year would be a subdued affair with only four guests. After supper on Christmas Eve, Paul was chatting to them in the guesthouse, which was now his responsibility. They had just heard Michel sound the bell for the Angelus when suddenly an armed man came in and shouted in Arabic for them to kneel down against the wall. Two others appeared, one of whom spoke French and introduced his companion as Sayah Attiyah, the local GIA *emir*. Michel, Amédée, Célestin and Jean-Pierre were quickly found and ordered over to the guesthouse, but

Amédée managed to slip away and hide in the cloister. Philippe Ranc, the community's sole novice, had been an army captain before he came to Atlas to try his vocation as a monk. His reactions were still fast: dragging with him his novice-master Christophe, he ran quickly down into the cellar where both of them hid in empty wine barrels. Attiyah next sent Paul to fetch "the Pope of this place". As Christian walked the short distance from his office, outwardly calm but inwardly sure that the moment of death was at hand, he repeated softly the meditation phrase which the Ribat had agreed to adopt at its latest meeting. It was the opening phrase of each of the Hours of the Divine Office: "O God come to my aid. O Lord make haste to help me".

"This is a house of peace," he said. "No one comes in here with weapons. If you want to discuss anything with us, come in, but leave your weapons outside. If that's not possible, we'll talk outside." Attiyah wasn't much more than twenty, but Christian knew he was a hardened killer, responsible for the massacre of the Croats. Nevertheless he agreed to step outside with the prior before presenting his demands. He wanted money, medical supplies, and a doctor to come and serve his fighters in the mountains. Christian refused on all counts. Firstly, the monks lived in poverty and had no money over and above their essential needs. Secondly, any medical supplies they had were only sufficient to maintain Luc's clinic, where they were given out as needed. Thirdly, the only doctor was

Luc, and he was far too old to go and live in the mountains. The GIA knew very well that if they needed treatment, they could come to the monastery for it: Luc had always treated anyone who came for help, without distinction and without asking awkward questions.

Attiyah blustered, "You have no choice!"

"Oh but I do have a choice."

The two continued to talk for about fifteen minutes. Eventually Christian protested, "We're getting ready to celebrate Christmas, which for us is the birth of the Prince of Peace - and you come in like this, with weapons ..."

"I'm sorry," replied Attiyah. "I didn't know." He was clearly embarrassed and agreed to come back another time - but when he did, he would expect from the monastery a definite agreement to assist the GIA. The three men then shook hands with everyone and quickly left. A shiver went down the spines of some of the monks when they thought that these hands might be the same ones which cut the throats of the Croats only ten days before.

To go or to stay

Luc had slept peacefully through everything; when he was told the GIA had come to take him away, he just shrugged his shoulders. It was decided not to report the incident to the police. What could they do, beyond harrassing the neighbours to show they were taking the matter seriously? Meanwhile, the most important business immediately at hand was to celebrate the birth of the Prince of Peace. At 10.30 pm Christian rang the bell for Vigils, which had been specially brought forward for Christmas and would be followed immediately by Midnight Mass. It was only when they heard the bell that Philippe and Christophe emerged from their hiding places, amazed to find everyone alive and unharmed.

On 26th December the community met to discuss what to do. Whatever happened, they must not allow themselves to be forced to channel money or supplies to the guerrillas. But what would happen when Attiyah, or his emissary, came back and met with a flat refusal? They had no desire to commit collective suicide, nor did they want to risk the lives of the Muslims who worked with them in the monastery. Presumably, therefore, they would have to leave. So they had better start planning how best to do it without attracting undue attention, and where to go - since they were determined to keep the community together. News of their decision spread quickly through the village grapevine, and one of the monks reported a comment he'd heard from a neighbour: "You still have a little escape door by which you can leave. We don't. No way out, no escape door." Mgr Henri Teissier, who had taken over as archbishop of Algiers on Duval's retirement, arrived to express his concern about the impact their departure would have on Christian morale in Algeria. Christian was also concerned about that, and he arranged

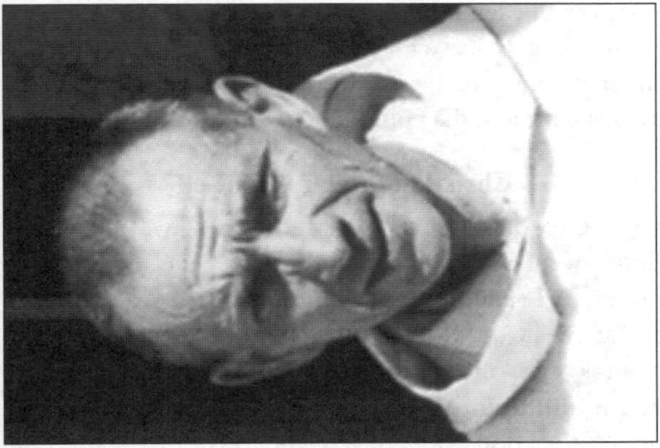

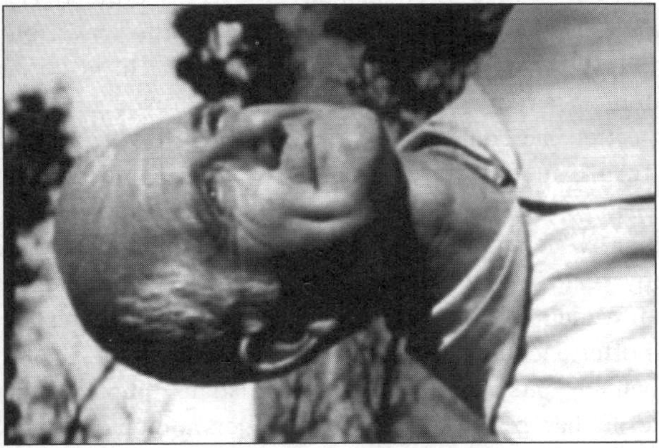

Brother Célestin (left) and Brother Bruno (right).

to speak with each brother individually: each one admitted he was not at peace with the decision to leave. A second chapter meeting resulted in a unanimous reveral of the previous decision: the community would stay.

Christian prepares himself

Two or three individuals *did* need to get away. Paul and Célestin were badly shaken up. It made sense for them to go over to France at least temporarily for a thorough medical check-up. Philippe was known to be yearning to get stuck into serious theological studies - so much so that the community had strong doubts whether the Trappist vocation was really right for him. At any rate, this seemed an excellent time to send him away somewhere where he could study in peace and quiet. The *wali* of Medea would have liked everyone to leave, but could not bring himself to order them to. He issued a statement saying that since they had refused military protection, he could not guarantee their safety. Christian in turn issued a statement: "If anything bad should happen to us, it would be unjust to hold responsible a country which has welcomed us with such kindness for so many years." On 30th December Cardinal Duval phoned from Algiers to express his delight at their resolve to stay, and offer encouragement: "The whole Church of Algeria is behind you!" On 1st January Christian completed the letter he had begun that night in Algiers a month before, and sent it to his brother Gérard in a sealed envelope, only to be opened should anything happen to him.

A birthday party for Luc

Paradoxically, the terrible events of Christmas night may have saved Célestin's life. Soon after reaching France he suffered a massive heart attack; it would have happened anyway, and in Algeria he would never have been able to get proper treatment in time, and would have died. Paul bounced back in fine form after a few weeks' holiday, in time for Luc's 80th birthday on 31st January. Luc was the only member of the community who seemed completely unconcerned about the danger: "What can happen to us? To go to see God and be bathed in his tenderness?" He couldn't expect to live much longer anyway, and he had already handed down instructions for when his time came - assuming of course that he would experience a natural and not-too-sudden death, since, "If it's death by violence, that's that." The others were to gather round his bed, read the Gospel story of the Prodigal Son and recite the Lord's Prayer - and finally open a bottle of champagne! Each day, Luc prayed: "Lord, give me the grace to die without hatred in my heart."

Christian prays for his enemies

Attiyah was killed the following month. Badly wounded after his unit was ambushed by the army, he had hidden up for nine days not far from Tibhirine before dying of his injuries. Christian tried to imagine how it must have been for someone with so much innocent blood on his hands to appear before the face of God. Since Christmas he had been praying for this man who had threatened his community. Now he pleaded with God for Attiyah's soul, making excuses for him: the *emir* had held back from killing the monks and, although he must have been in agony all those days, he had not compromised the monastery by sending for help.

Dangers increase

For the past twenty years Jean-Pierre had driven to Medea three times a week, to market the garden produce and do the shopping. Now, the drive each way was full of fear: there was no knowing what might happen on the road. Even so, he told Christian he would carry on; he'd made friends with so many of the Muslim shopkeepers, and would miss not seeing them. The prior did install a freezer so he could cut down the frequency of his journeys. Yet despite its isolation and apparent vulnerability, Tibhirine was as safe if not safer than the capital: Attiyah was believed to have extended his *aman* (promise of protection) to the monastery, and after his death the local GIA continued to respect it. When, for the first time, a priest and a Sister were assassinated, it was in Algiers in broad daylight. Their deaths hit the international headlines.

Fr Henri Vergès, one of the Ribat's founder members, was particularly well-known to the Atlas community, but the grieving monks urged the importance of getting the killings into perspective: thousands of ordinary Algerians had been slain, as had at least fifty *imams* who refused to give their moral support to the extremists' 'religious war'. Michel commented: "'Martyr' - that's a rather ambiguous word around here... If anything should happen to us, though I hope nothing does, we want to live it here, in solidarity with all the Algerian men and women who have already paid with their lives. We just want to stand side by side with all the unknown victims." Christian, recalling the medics executed in Medea, insisted: "Christians are not the only martyrs of charity. Muslims are, too."

Staying put amid anarchy

After two Augustinian Sisters were killed in October, a number of religious congregations decided to pull out. The White Fathers chose to remain, and on 27th December four of them were killed in Tizi-Ouzou. Every six months the brothers of Atlas met together to review their decision to remain, and each time it was unanimously reaffirmed. No rational calculations were involved, only the conviction that - for the time being at least - this was where God wanted them to be. The chapter room where the community meetings were held was very simply furnished: a square table covered with a handwoven Berber cloth, and on the wall a reproduction of Roublev's Trinity - an evocative reminder that God himself is community. The eight brothers - Christian, Luc, Célestin, Christophe, Michel, Paul, Jean-Pierre and Amédée - usually gathered there each morning for Terce, and again each evening between dinner and Compline, shelling peas or filling lavender sachets while Christian gave them a digest of the day's news which he had heard on the radio. As their beloved Algeria dissolved into anarchy, they came to depend more and more on the support of their life as a community: the daily round of work and prayer and mutual forbearance through which God was present to them.

Lent 1995 - the action of grace

In a circular letter of April 1995, sent out to all their friends and well-wishers, Christian wrote: "At the beginning of Lent we set aside time for a long sharing on the theme: 'During the past eighteen months, what changes have there been within us and between us?' On the face of it nothing had changed: same places, same people! And yet... although our characters remained the same - our nice side and our rough edges - there was among us a new quality of harmony and mutual acceptance. We'd achieved a greater capacity to listen, thanks to the overwhelming need to work out decisions, and the obvious fact that we had to go forward step by step, in faith. Afterwards, we had a strong feeling of having been inspired and, as it were, accompanied. The danger is there every day, everywhere. Each one knows this, feels this, for himself and for the whole environment in which we are living. The action of grace is also there every day..."

Essential medicines in Algeria were constantly running out, but Luc always had what he needed. Packages came from donors all over France, Germany and Switzerland, and the Algerian authorities had arranged with the customs officers to let them through automatically without delay. But for a long time no packages had arrived, and he was almost out of everything. He told Christian he was praying desperately to Marthe Robin who, when he visited her home nearly forty years before, had promised him his medical supplies would never run out. Next day a package arrived.

All shall be well - Alleluia!

On 15th March 1996 Luc wrote in a letter to a friend, "I entered my 83rd year in January. An old man is a miserable thing unless there's a song in his soul. Pray that I will remain in joy."

Bruno hadn't been to Tibhirine for years: he was really looking forward to seeing the 'motherhouse' again. Shortly before he set off from Fez, on 18th March, the gardener Thami begged him to cancel the trip, saying he'd had a premonition. Bruno knew the situation in Algeria only too well. However Christian's second six-year term in office was due to end soon, and Bruno needed to be present for the election which was scheduled for Palm Sunday, 31st March. Christian planned to step down and was hoping that Christophe, who was already serving as sub-prior, would be elected. But the other monks thought Christophe still too young and quick-tempered; it was more likely that Christian would be re-elected. Next day was the Feast of St Joseph, and Fr Carmona had arranged to celebrate his name-day the best way he knew, by spending it at Atlas. Very much to his surprise the brothers had prepared a party for him. They presented him with a copy of the Revelations of Divine Love by the mediaeval English anchoress Julian of Norwich; on the flyleaf they had stamped the monastery seal, and written in bright red letters "All shall be well - Alleluia!"

Ribat group gathers March 1996

No Ribat meeting had been held for two years, but despite the ongoing insecurity one had been arranged for this spring: the group needed it so much. Three priests and nine women religious arrived on the Feast of the Annunciation, Monday 25th March. Paul also returned that day from France, where he'd been to visit his sick mother. He traveled via Medea, where he stopped off to see an elderly woman friend, but insisted he mustn't stay very long: "Anything could happen. I'm in a rush to get back with my brothers." He arrived in Tibhirine early in the evening, beaming all over his face and bringing presents for everyone: a book on sufism for Christian, a cheese with the distinctive Tamié label of a red Savoyard cross, and several boxes of chocolates which he put in his room ready to share round at Easter.

The last night

The Ribat group had spent the day in discussion and reflection. The members present numbered a healthy fifteen since, besides Christian, Christophe was now a regular participant, and so was Michel. The other brothers still usually avoided the discussion sessions, but joined in the prayer times. Christian was very late getting to bed that night: the light in his office remained on for some time as he prepared material for the following day. Since Christmas 1993 he had taken to sleeping in his office, on the ground floor, to be on hand if anything happened. Amédée and Luc also had their bedrooms on the ground floor, near the entrance, as did Jean-Pierre who served as night porter. All the other bedrooms were on the first floor.

Armed men break into the compound

About 1.00 am two men knocked at the lodge and demanded to see the *toubib*. Mohammed explained that Luc didn't see patients at night, whereupon the men insisted and became threatening. They swung themselves up on the door, broke the fanlight and shone their lamp into the passageway calling "Moha, Moha!". This was what his friends called him - but he didn't know these people, and he could tell from their accents that they weren't local. His wife begged him not to leave the house, but he decided he should go and tell the monks what was happening. Slipping as quietly as possible into the courtyard, he found it full of armed men: about twenty of them had climbed over the wall while he was talking at the door. Their leader, a man with red hair, ordered him to fetch the "seven monks". He was clearly acting on information received that there should be *seven*; Mohammed was careful not to let on that there were eight, plus Bruno from Fez who made nine. The raiders were not wearing masks, and he realised with a shiver that this could mean they intended to kill him, and any other witnesses.

The seven monks rounded up

Jean-Pierre was woken by the sound of voices in the corridor. The door to his room had a glass panel covered by a curtain; peering round the edge of the curtain he saw a man wearing a turban and carrying a gun walking towards the prior's office. A moment later he heard Christian's voice: "Which of you is in charge?" Luc came out of his room, carrying his medical bag, and Christian went outside with him. Jean-Pierre realised that the 'brothers of the mountains' were paying another nocturnal visit, presumably because they required medical services.

Hopefully Christian would sort it out. He stayed quietly in his room, praying. Meanwhile some of the other raiders went upstairs with Mohammed and routed Christophe, Célestin, Michel, Paul and Bruno out of their rooms. The priest-guests were occupying some spare rooms further along the corridor, and when Fr Thierry Becker heard noises he came to investigate. Seeing the intervening door open a crack, Mohammed quickly caught Fr Becker's eye with a warning glance which sent him back. As they were going downstairs one of the raiders stumbled; Mohammed seized his chance, slipped away and ran out into the darkness. A guerrilla tried to open the door to Amédée's room, but when he realised it was locked let it be: they already had their seven. Through the keyhole, Amédée watched them pillage Luc's room. Then they disappeared, and silence fell again on the monastery.

Waiting for dawn

Going upstairs to check that the priests were safe, Amédée found Fr Becker and told him what had happened, then knocked on Jean-Pierre's door and broke the news to him. The three conducted a quick search of the premises. They found everything in Christian's office overturned, his camera and typewriter missing, and the telephone wires cut. In Paul's room the raiders seemed to have helped themselves to the chocolates, throwing the wrappings on the floor. A box of liqueur chocolates lay untouched because of the Islamic prohibition on alcohol, so Fr Becker put it in the fridge to await Paul's return. The Tamié cheese had been taken but then thrown away in the corridor - perhaps because of the cross on the label. The three prayed the rosary together, then snatched a couple of hours' sleep before Vigils at 5.15, for which they were joined by another of the priest-guests. After Vigils they sat and waited for daybreak. They expected to hear the call to prayer, but it didn't come: the villagers already knew what had happened, and they were too frightened to come to the mosque. Once it was fully light Jean-Pierre and Fr Becker drove to Medea, to report the abduction to the police and phone Archbishop Teissier.

The rest of the Ribat guests departed for Algiers, but Fr Becker stayed. The two remaining monks, both in their seventies, seemed amazingly calm and at peace. However they needed someone to help them deal with the authorities: Jean-Pierre's Arabic wasn't up to it, and Amédée was so deaf that even with two hearing aids he couldn't always follow what was being said. Also, neither of them knew how to cook, but when Fr Becker went to the kitchen to fix something he found a large pot of soup and another of beans sitting on the stove, ready to be heated up. Luc had got up in the middle of the night, as he so often did because his asthma kept him awake, and prepared the next day's meal. Late that afternoon, when the police had finished searching the monastery, a neighbour came to hand over Michel's white prayer cowl; he had picked it up a few hundred yards along a mountain track. No other trace either of the monks or their captors was to be found. Amédée, Jean-Pierre and Fr Becker spent the night at Medea's best hotel, at police expense and with a police guard posted outside the door. The following day they returned to the monastery to pack up their personal belongings before departing for Algiers.

Communiqué 43

For almost a month nothing was heard, but on 18th April a message appeared fly-posted on walls around Tibhirine. The full text of the GIA's 'Communiqué 43' was published a week later in London. A lengthy document, much of it was taken up with attempts to justify the abduction of the Trappists against widespread moral indignation within the Islamic world, and even within other GIA factions. It ended with an offer to return the monks safe and sound in return for the liberation of imprisoned GIA leaders: "The choice is yours - release for release. If you refuse, we will cut their throats."

Message from Christian

Archbishop Teissier was asked to come to the French Embassy in Algiers to listen to an audio-tape which had been delivered by a GIA emissary. "This is Brother Christian, son of Monique and Guy de Chergé, aged 59, monk of the monastery of Tibhirine and prior of the community. Today is Saturday 20th April, and it is 11.00 pm." Christian's voice on the tape sounded completely calm. He proceeded to give some of the day's news, to prove he was speaking on the date given. Then, "We are informing you that we are being held as hostages, alive and in good health, by the GIA fighters." Next, each of the others spoke in turn, following the same formula. Teissier, who knew the monks well, confirmed that these were their voices. Finally the kidnappers, who could be heard in the background, gave the microphone back to Christian. This time he sounded different, as if he was being made to say something he didn't want to say: "They are holding us as hostages, and they demand that the French government release a certain number of hostages belonging to the group in exchange for our freedom. This exchange offer would appear to be non-negotiable."

Worldwide prayers

In mosques throughout Algeria, prayers were being offered for the monks' safety. The Pope remembered them during an Eastertide Mass celebrated in Tunis: "May the risen Christ grant them to see their trial end with their release! May God sustain the Church's hope in this country and guide the Algerian people on the path of peace and reconciliation!" At the Cathedral of Notre Dame in Paris, Cardinal Lustiger presided at a gathering of 2,500, including representatives of the Muslim, Jewish and Protestant communities in France. During this service, which was televised, seven candles brought from Atlas were solemnly lit, to remain burning until the monks were set free. Similar prayer vigils took place all over France. On 7th May Muslim leaders in Paris issued a *fatwa* condemning the indiscriminate violence of the GIA, and the abduction of the monks. "Dragging them into this political business shows the incapacity and weakness of their abductors, because they have picked on unarmed men without any means of protection... God says: 'Whoever kills a man who himself has neither killed, nor committed violence upon the earth, will be considered as one who has killed all men; and whoever saves a single man will be considered as having saved all men.' (*Koran, sura V, verse 32*)"

Communiqué 44 - we have cut their throats

On 23rd May a radio news-reader cautiously announced receipt of a message from the GIA - though the station had no means of verifying its authenticity. 'Communiqué 44', dated two days previously, stated that negotiations with the authorities had broken down, and therefore: "We have cut the throats of the seven monks". At his home in Algiers, 92 and confined to bed following an operation, Cardinal Duval told his niece he felt "crucified" by the news. He died a week later, on the very day when the

Algerian police announced that the monks' remains had been found. In Paris, Cardinal Lustiger solemnly extinguished the seven candles: "We pray for all those who have died in these massacres, for all those whom the monks did not wish to abandon. I am sure that at the last moment, they forgave. Their death must be a sign of hope: love is stronger than hatred. All those who can, I ask to go on praying for peace in Algeria."

TESTAMENT OF CHRISTIAN DE CHERGÉ

Unsealing the letter which Christian had sent him for safekeeping two years before, Gérard called his mother and the rest of the family together, and read it out to them. They agreed unanimously that they should not keep it for themselves alone, but share it with the whole world.

When an 'A-Dieu' takes on a face

"If it should happen one day - and it could be today - that I become a victim of the terrorism which now seems ready to engulf all the foreigners living in Algeria, I would like my community, my Church, my family, to remember that my life was *given* to God and to this country. I ask them to accept that the Sole Master of all life was not a stranger to this brutal departure. I ask them to pray for me - for how could I be found worthy of such an offering? I ask them to be able to link this death with the many other deaths which were just as violent, but forgotten through indifference and anonymity. My life has no more value than any other. Nor any less value. In any case it has not the innocence of childhood. I have lived long enough to know that I am an accomplice in the evil which seems, alas, to prevail in the world, even in that which would strike me blindly. I should like, when the time comes, to have the moment of lucidity which would allow me to beg forgiveness of God and of my fellow human beings, and at the same time to forgive with all my heart the one who would strike me down.

I could not desire such a death. It seems to me important to state this. I do not see, in fact, how I could rejoice if the people I love were to be accused indiscriminately of my murder. To owe it to an Algerian, whoever he may be, would be too high a price to pay for what will, perhaps, be called the 'grace of martyrdom,' especially if he says he is acting in fidelity to what he believes to be Islam. I am aware of the scorn which can be heaped on Algerians indiscriminately. I am also aware of the caricatures of Islam which a certain islamism encourages. It is too easy to salve one's conscience by identifying this religious way with the fundamentalist ideologies of the extremists. For me, Algeria and Islam are something different: they are a body and a soul. I have proclaimed this often enough, I believe, in the sure knowledge of what I have received from it, finding there so often that true strand of the Gospel, learnt at my mother's knee, my very first Church, already in Algeria itself, in the respect of believing Muslims. My death, clearly, will appear to justify those who hastily judged me naive, or idealistic: 'Let him tell us now what he thinks of it!' But these people must realise that my avid curiosity will then be satisfied. This is what I shall be able to do, if God wills - immerse my gaze in that of the Father, and contemplate with him his children of Islam just as he sees them, all shining with the glory of Christ, the fruit of His Passion, filled with the Gift of the Spirit, whose secret joy will always be to establish communion, and to refashion the likeness, playfully delighting in the differences.

For this life lost, totally mine and totally theirs, I thank God who seems to have willed it entirely for the sake of that joy in everything and in spite of everything. In this *thank you,* which sums up everything in my life to this moment, I certainly include you, friends of yesterday and today, and you, my friends of this place, along with my mother and father, my sisters and brothers and their families, the hundredfold granted as was promised! And also you, the friend of my final moment, who would not be aware of what you were doing. Yes, I also say this *Thank You* and this A-Dieu to you, in whom I see the face of God. And may we find each other, happy good thieves, in Paradise, if it pleases God, the Father of us both. Amen! (In sha'Allah) ."

Algiers, December 1, 1993 - Tibhirine, January 1, 1994
Christian.

Sources

- *Osservatore Romano* (English edition): 16 September 1985; 17 April 1996
- *Cistercian Studies Quarterly: "Atlas Martyrs"*, Donald McGlynn OCSO (32.2, 1997 p. 149); *"The Wider Horizon of the Algeria of the Heart"*, Julian Doherty OCSO (32.2, 1997 p. 195); *"Monk, Martyr and Mystic: Christian de Chergé (1937-1996)"*, Bernardo Olivera OCSO (34.3, 1999 p. 321)
- *"Modern Algeria"*, John Ruedy (Indiana University Press, 1992)
- *"Abd El-Kader"*, Smaïl Aouli, Ramdane Redjala, Philippe Zoummeroff (Fayard, 1994)
- *"Les Martyrs de Tibhirine"*, Mireille Duteil (Éditions Brepols, 1996)
- *"Sept vies pour Dieu et l'Algérie"*, Bruno Chenu ed. (Bayard Éditions/ Centurion, 1996)
- *"How Far to Follow?"* Bernard Olivera (St Bede's Publications, 1997)
- *"A Heritage Too Big for Us"*, Donald McGlynn OCSO (Nunraw Abbey, 1997)
- *"Tibhirine - les veilleurs de l'Atlas"*, Robert Masson (Cerf/ Saint-Augustin, 1997)

- *"Le Cardinal Duval: un homme d'espérance en Algérie"*, Marie-Christine Ray (Les Éditions du Cerf, 1998)
- *"Christian de Chergé: Prieur de Tibhirine"*, Marie-Christine Ray (Bayard Éditions/ Centurion, 1999)
- *"Si nous nous taisons ...Le martyre des moines de Tibhirine"*, René Guitton (Calmann-Lévy, 2001)
- *"Au nom de la vérité: Algérie 1954-1962"*, Léon-Étienne Duval (Albin Michel, 2001)
- *"The Monks of Tibhirine - Faith, Love and Terror in Algeria"*, John W Kiser (St Martin's Press, 2002)

Informative Catholic Reading

We hope that you have enjoyed reading this booklet.

If you would like to find out more about CTS booklets - we'll send you our free information pack and catalogue.

Please send us your details:

Name ....

Address ....

....

....

Postcode ....

Telephone..

Email ....

Send to: CTS, 40-46 Harleyford Road,
Vauxhall, London
SE11 5AY

Tel: 020 7640 0042
Fax: 020 7640 0046
Email: info@cts-online.org.uk

CTS